# Last Judgment Continued

# Last Judgment Continued
by Emanuel Swedenborg
Translated by John Whitehead

I. THE LAST JUDGMENT HAS BEEN ACCOMPLISHED. In the former small work on The Last Judgment, the following subjects were treated of: The day of the Last Judgment does not mean the destruction of the world. The procreations of the human race will never cease. Heaven and hell are from the human race. All who have ever been born men from the beginning of creation, and are deceased, are either in heaven or in hell. The Last Judgment must be where all are together; therefore in the spiritual world, and not on the earth. The Last Judgment exists when the end of the church is; and the end of the church is when there is no faith, because there is no charity. All the things which are predicted in the Apocalypse are at this day fulfilled. The Last Judgment has been accomplished. Babylon and its destruction. The former heaven and its abolition. The state of the world and of the church hereafter.

The subject of the Last Judgment is continued, principally that it may be known what the state of the world and the church was before the Last Judgment, and what the state of the world and the church has become since; also, how the Last Judgment was accomplished upon the Reformed.

It is a common opinion in the Christian world, that the whole heaven we see, and the whole earth inhabited by men will perish at the day of the Last Judgment, and that a new heaven and a new earth will exist in their places; that the souls of men will then receive their bodies, and that man will thus again be man as before. This opinion has become a matter of faith, because the Word has not been understood otherwise than according to the sense of its letter; and it could not be understood otherwise, until its spiritual sense was disclosed, also, because by many the belief has been acquired that the soul is only a breath exhaled by man; and that spirits, as well as angels, are of the substance of wind. While there was such a deficiency of understanding concerning souls, and concerning spirits and angels, the Last Judgment could not be thought of in any other manner. But when it comes to be understood, that a man is a man after death, just as he was a man in the world, with the sole difference that then he is clothed with a spiritual body, and not as before with a natural body; and that the spiritual body appears before those who are spiritual, even as the natural body appears before those who are natural, it may then also be understood, that the Last Judgment will not be in the natural, but in the spiritual world; for all the men who were ever born and have died, are together there.

When this is understood, then may the paradoxes be dissipated, which man would otherwise think concerning the state of souls after death, and their reunion with putrid corpses, and concerning the destruction of the created universe, thus concerning the Last Judgment. The paradoxes concerning the state of souls after death that he would think are these: That man would then be like an exhalation, or like wind, or like ether; either that he would be floating in the air, or not abiding in any place, but in a somewhere, which they call Pu; and that he would see nothing, because he had no eyes; hear nothing, because he had no ears; speak nothing, because he had no mouth; and would therefore be blind, deaf, and dumb; and continually in the expectation, which could not but be sad, of receiving again at the day of the Last Judgment, those functions of the soul from which all the delight of life proceeds. Also that the souls of all who have lived since the first creation, must be in a like miserable state, and that the men who lived fifty or sixty centuries ago, were likewise still floating in the air, or remaining in Pu, and awaiting judgment; besides other lamentable things.

I pass over paradoxes, similar to, and equally numerous with these, which the man who does not know that he is a man after death as before, must think concerning the destruction of the universe. But when he knows that a man after death is not an exhalation or a wind, but a spirit, and if he has lived well, an angel in heaven, and that spirits and angels are men in a perfect form, can then think from his understanding concerning the state of man after death, and the Last Judgment, and not from faith separate from the understanding, from which mere traditions go forth: and he may also with certainty conclude from his understanding, that the Last Judgment, which is predicted in the Word, will not exist in the natural world, but in the spiritual world, where all are together: and furthermore, that whenever it does exist, it must be revealed, for the sake of belief in the Word.

Put away from you the idea that the soul is like an exhalation, and then think of your own state, or of the state of your friends, or of the state of your infants after death. Will you not think that you will live a man, and they likewise? And since there is no life which is life without the senses, you cannot think otherwise than that they also see, hear, and speak; thus also panegyrists write over the deceased, placing them in heaven among the angels, in white garments, and in paradises. But if afterwards you relapse into the idea, that the soul is an exhalation, and has no sensitive life until after the Last Judgment, can you help being distracted when you think, What and where shall I be in the meantime? Shall I float in the air, or remain in Pu? 6-1 Yet the preacher teaches me that after death I shall come among the happy, if I have believed well and lived well. You may believe then, as the truth is, that you are a man after death as well as before it, with only the difference that there is between the natural and the spiritual. Thus also all those think who believe in eternal life, and know nothing of this hypothetical tradition concerning the soul.

From what has been said already, it may appear that the Last Judgment cannot exist in the natural world, but in the spiritual world. That it also has existed there, may be seen from the things related of it from sight, in the former small work on The Last Judgment , and still further from the particulars about to be related from sight, of the Last Judgment upon the Reformed. He who attends may also see it from the new things which are now revealed concerning heaven, the Word, and the church. What man can draw such things from himself?

II. THE STATE OF THE WORLD AND OF THE CHURCH BEFORE THE LAST JUDGMENT, AND AFTER IT. That the Last Judgment has been accomplished in the spiritual world, may appear from what has just been said. Nevertheless, in order to know anything of the state of the world and the church before and after it, it is altogether necessary that the following things should be known: I. What is meant by "the former heaven" and "the former earth" which passed away (Apoc. 21:1). II. Who, and of what quality were those who were in the former heaven and in the former earth. III. Before the Last Judgment was effected upon them much of the communication between heaven and the world, thus also between the Lord and the church, was intercepted. IV. After the Last Judgment the communication was restored. V. Hence it is, that after the Last Judgment, and not before, revelations were made for the New Church. VI. The state of the world and of the church before the Last Judgment was like evening and night, but after it like morning and day.

I. What is meant by "the former heaven" and "the former earth" which passed away, mentioned in the Apocalypse (21:1) "The former heaven" and "the former earth" there mentioned, does not mean the heaven visible to the eyes of men in the world, nor the earth which is inhabited by men; nor the former heaven, in which all those are who have lived well since the first creation. But congregations of spirits are meant who had made seeming heavens between heaven and hell for themselves, and because all spirits and angels dwell upon lands, as well as men, therefore by "the former heaven" and "the former earth," these are meant. The passing away of that heaven and that earth was seen, and it has been described from sight in the work on The Last Judgment.

II. Who, and of what quality were those who were in "the former heaven," and "the former earth," was described in the small work on The Last Judgment; but because the understanding of what follows depends on the knowledge of who they were and their quality, something shall here be said concerning them. All those who gathered themselves together under heaven, and in various places formed seeming heavens for themselves, and also called them heavens, were conjoined with the angels of the lowest heaven, but only as to externals, not as to internals. For the most part they were the goats and those akin to them, who are named in Matthew (25:41-46); who indeed, in the world had not done evils, for they had lived well morally; but they had not done goods from a good origin, for they had separated faith from charity, and hence had not regarded evils as sins. Because they had lived as Christians in externals, they were conjoined with the angels of the lowest heaven, who were like them in externals, but not like them in internals; they being "the sheep," and in faith, yet in the faith of charity. On account of this conjunction they were necessarily tolerated; for to separate them, before the Last Judgment, would have brought injury upon those who were in the lowest heaven, who would have been drawn into destruction with them. This is what the Lord foretold in Matthew: Jesus spoke a parable; the kingdom of the heaven is like unto a man who sowed good seed in his field; but while men slept, his enemy came, and sowed tares, and went away; when the blade was sprung up, and brought forth fruit, then appeared the tares also; so the servants of the householder coming, said unto him, Lord, didst not thou sow good seed in thy field? Wilt thou then that we go and gather them up? But he said, Nay, lest, while ye gather up the tares, ye root up at the same time the wheat with them: let both grow together until the harvest; and in the time of harvest I will say to the reapers, Gather ye together first the tares, and bind them in bundles to burn them; but gather the wheat into my barn. He who hath sown the good seed, is the Son of man; the field is the world; the seed are the sons of the kingdom; the tares are the sons of evil; the harvest is the consummation of the age; as therefore the tares are gathered together, and burned, so shall it be in the consummation of the age (Matt. 13:24-30, 37-40).

"The consummation of the age" is the last time of the church; "the tares" are those who are interiorly evil; "the wheat" are those who are interiorly good; "the gathering together in bundles to burn," is the Last Judgment upon them; that harm should not be done to the good by separation before the Last Judgment, is signified by "lest in gathering up the tares, ye root up at the same time the wheat with them: let both grow until the harvest."

III. Before the Last Judgment was effected upon them, much of the communication between heaven and the world, thus between the Lord and the church, was intercepted. All enlightenment comes to man from the Lord through heaven, and it enters by an internal way. So long as there were congregations of such spirits between heaven and the world, or between the Lord and the church, man could not be enlightened. It was as when a sunbeam is cut off by a black interposing cloud, or as when the sun is eclipsed, and its light arrested, by the interjacent moon. Wherefore, if anything had been then revealed by the Lord, either it would not have been understood, or if understood, still it would not have been received, or if received, still it would afterwards have been suffocated. Now since all these interposing congregations were dissipated by the Last Judgment, it is plain, IV. That the communication between heaven and the world, or between the Lord and the church, has been restored.

V. Hence it is, that after the Last Judgment has been accomplished, and not before, revelations were made for the New Church. For since communication has been restored by the Last Judgment, man can be enlightened and reformed; that is, can understand the Divine truth of the Word, receive it when understood, and retain it when received, for the interposing obstacles are removed; and therefore John, after the former heaven and the former earth passed away, said that: He saw a New Heaven and a New Earth, and then, the holy city Jerusalem, descending from God out of heaven, prepared as a Bride before her Husband; and he heard the One sitting upon the throne, say, Behold, I make all things new (Apoc. 21:1, 2, 5). That the church is meant by "Jerusalem" may be seen in The Doctrine Concerning the Lord. Concerning its new things.

VI. The state of the world and of the church before the Last Judgment was like evening and night, but after it, like morning and day. When the light of truth does not appear, and truth is not received, there is a state of the church in the world like evening and night; that there was a state before the Last Judgment, may appear from what is said above ; but when the light of truth appears, and the truth is received, there is a state of the church in the world like morning and day. Hence it is, that these two states of the church are called "evening and morning" and "night and day," in the Word; as in the following passages: The Holy One said unto me, Until the evening the morning two thousand three hundred; then shall the sanctuary be justified (Dan. 8:14). The vision of the evening and the morning is truth (Dan. 8:26). There shall be one day, which is known to Jehovah, neither day nor night, for about the time of evening there shall be light (Zech. 14:7). One crying unto me out of Seir, Watchman, what of the night? The watchman said, The morning cometh, and also the night (Isa. 21:11, 12). Concerning the last time of the church, Jesus said: Watch, for ye know not when the Lord of the house will come, whether at evening, at midnight, at cock-crowing, or in the morning (Mark 13:35). Jesus said, I must work while it is day; the night cometh, when no one can work (John 9:4); and elsewhere (as in Isa. 17:14; Jer. 6:4, 5; Ps. 30:6; 65:9; 90:6). Since such things are meant by "evening and night," therefore the Lord, in order to fulfil the Word, also was buried in the evening and afterward rose again in the morning.

III. THE LAST JUDGMENT UPON THE REFORMED. In the former small work on The Last Judgment it treated of the judgment upon those who are meant by Babylon; and something of the judgment upon the Mohammedans and upon the Gentiles; but not of the judgment upon the Reformed. It was said only, that the Reformed were in the middle, arranged there according to countries; the Papists around them; the Mohammedans around the Papists, and around these the Gentiles and peoples of various religions. The Reformed constituted the middle, or central region, because the Word is read by them and the Lord is worshiped, and hence with them there is the greatest light; and spiritual light, which is from the Lord as a sun, which in its essence is the Divine love, proceeds and extends itself on every side, and enlightens even those who are in the extreme circumferences, and opens the faculty of understanding truths, as far as from their religion they can receive them. For spiritual light in its essence is the Divine wisdom, and it enters the understanding in man, as far as, from knowledges received, he has the faculty of perceiving it; and it does not pass through spaces, like the light of the world, but through the affections and perceptions of truth, therefore, in an instant, to the last limits of the heavens. From these are the appearances of spaces in that world. Concerning these things more may be seen in The Doctrine Concerning the Sacred Scripture.

The Last Judgment upon the Reformed shall be described in the following order. I. Upon whom of the Reformed the Last Judgment was effected. II. The signs and visitations before the Last Judgment. III. How the universal judgment was effected. IV. The salvation of the sheep.

I. Upon whom among the Reformed the Last Judgment was effected. The Last Judgment was effected upon those only of the Reformed, who in the world confessed God, read the Word, heard preaching, partook of the sacrament of the Supper, and did not neglect the solemnities of the worship of the church; and yet thought that adulteries, various kinds of theft, lying, revenge, hatred, and the like, were allowable. These although they confessed God, still made no account of sins against Him; they read the Word, and still they made no account of the precepts of life in it; they heard preachings, and still they paid no attention to them; they went to the sacrament of the Supper, and still they did not desist from the evils of their former life; they did not neglect the solemnities of worship, and still they amended their lives in nothing. Thus they lived as if from religion, in their externals, yet in their internals they had nothing of it. These are they who are meant by "the dragon" in the Apocalypse (chap. 12); for it is there said of the dragon, that it was seen in heaven, that it fought with Michael in heaven, and that it drew down the third part of the stars from heaven; which things are said, because these, by means of the confession of God, by reading the Word, and by external worship, communicated with heaven. The same are meant by "the goats" in Matthew, chap. 25; to whom it is not said that they did evils, but that they omitted to do goods; and all such omit to do goods which are goods, because they do not shun evils as sins, and although they do not do them, still they think them allowable, and thus do them in spirit, and also in body, when permitted.

Upon all these from the Reformed the Last Judgment was effected, but not upon those who did not believe in God, who contemned the Word, and rejected from their hearts the holy things of the church; for all these, when they came from the natural world into the spiritual world, were cast into hell.

All who lived like Christians in externals, and made no account of the Christian life, made one exteriorly with the heavens, but interiorly with the hells, and since they could not be torn away in a moment from their conjunction with heaven, they were detained in the world of spirits, which is midway between heaven and hell, and it was permitted them to form societies, and to live together as in the world; and there by arts unknown to the world, to cause splendid appearances, and by this means to persuade themselves and others, that they were in heaven; therefore, from that external appearance they called their societies heavens. The heavens and the earths upon which they dwelt, are meant by "the former heaven, and the former earth which passed away" (Apoc. 21:1).

Meanwhile, so long as they remained there, the interiors of their minds were closed, and the exteriors were opened; by which means, their evils, by which they made one with the hells: did not appear. But when the Last Judgment was at hand, their interiors were disclosed, and they then appeared before all such as they really were; and since they then acted in unity with the hells, they were no longer able to simulate the Christian life, but from delight rushed into evils and crimes of every kind, and were turned into devils, and, moreover, were seen as such, some black, some fiery, and some livid like corpses; those who were in the pride of their own intelligence, appearing black; those who were in the insane love of ruling over all, appearing fiery; and those who were in the neglect and contempt of truth, appearing livid like corpses. Thus were the scenes of those theaters changed.

The Reformed constitute the inmost or middle part of the world of spirits, which is midway between heaven and hell, and are there arranged according to countries. In the center of this middle region are the English; towards the south and the east of it are the Dutch; towards the north, the Germans; towards the west and the north, the Swedes; and towards the west, the Danes. But those only who have lived the life of charity, and its faith, are in that middle region: many societies of them dwell there. Surrounding them are those of the Reformed, who have not lived the life of faith and charity: these are they who made as it were heavens to themselves. But there is a different arrangement of all in heaven, and also of all in hell. The reason why the Reformed constitute the middle there is, because with them the Word is read, and the Lord is also worshiped, from which the greatest light is there; and thence, as from a center, this light is propagated to all the circumferences and enlightens. For the light in which spirits and angels are, proceeds from the Lord as a sun, and this sun, in its essence, is the Divine love, and the light which proceeds from it in its essence is the Divine wisdom: all the spiritual of that world is derived from it. Concerning the Lord as the sun in the spiritual world, and concerning the light and heat of that sun, see the work on Heaven and Hell.

Every arrangement of the societies in that world, is an arrangement according to the differences of love; the reason of which is, that love is the life of man, and the Lord, who is Divine love itself, arranges them according to its reception; and the differences of loves are innumerable, which no one knows but the Lord alone. He so conjoins the societies, that they all lead as it were one life of man; the societies of the heavens one life of celestial and spiritual love; the societies of the hells, one life of diabolical and infernal love; He conjoins the heavens and the hells by oppositions. Because there is such an arrangement, every man after death goes into the society of his own love, nor can he go into any other, for his love opposes it. Hence it is that they who are in spiritual love are in heaven, but they who are in natural love only, are in hell. Spiritual love is implanted solely by the life of charity, and natural love remains natural, if the life of charity is omitted; and natural love, if it is not subjected to spiritual love, is opposed to it.

From these things it may appear, upon whom of the Reformed the Last Judgment was effected; that it was not upon those who were in the center, but upon those who were around it; who from external morality, as was said, appeared exteriorly like Christians, but interiorly they were not Christians, because they had no spiritual life.

II. The signs and visitations before the Last Judgment. There was seen above those who had formed to themselves seeming heavens as it were a storm cloud, which appearance was from the presence of the Lord in the angelic heavens above them, especially from His presence in the lowest heaven, lest any of them on account of the conjunction should be carried away and perish with them. The higher heavens moreover were brought down nearer to them, by which the interiors of those upon whom the judgment was about to come were disclosed; on which disclosure, they appeared no longer like moral Christians, as before, but like demons. They were tumultuous and strove among themselves about God, the Lord, the Word, faith, and the church; and because their lusts for evils were then also set free, they rejected all these things with contempt and ridicule, and rushed into every kind of enormity. Thus the state of those heavenly inhabitants was changed. Then at the same time all their splendid appearances, which they had made for themselves by arts unknown in the world, vanished away; their palaces were turned into vile huts; their gardens into stagnant pools; their temples into heaps of rubbish; and the very hills upon which they dwelt, into gravel heaps, and into other similar things, which corresponded to their wicked minds and lusts. For all the visible things of the spiritual world are correspondences of the affections of spirits and angels. These were the signs of the coming judgment.

As the disclosure of the interiors increased, so the order among the inhabitants was changed and inverted. Those who were most powerful in reasonings against the holy things of the church, rushed into the middle, and assumed the dominion; and the rest, who were less powerful in reasonings, receded to the circumferences, and acknowledged those who were in the middle as their tutor-angels. Thus they collected themselves together into the form of hell.

These changes of their state were accompanied

by various concussions of their dwellings and lands; which were followed by earthquakes, mighty according to their perversions. Here and there, too, chasms were made towards the hells which were under them, and a communication was thus opened with them. Exhalations were then seen ascending like smoke mingled with sparks of fire. These also were signs which preceded, which are also meant by the Lord's words concerning the consummation of the age, and then concerning the Last Judgment, in the Evangelists: Nation shall be stirred up against nation; there shall be great earthquakes in divers places; signs also from heaven, terrible and great. And there shall be distress of nations, the sea and the billows roaring (Luke 21:10, 11, 25; Matt. 24:7; Mark 13:8).

Visitations also were made by angels; for before any ill conditioned society perishes, visitation always precedes. The angels exhorted them to desist, and denounced destruction upon them if they did not. Then they also sought out and separated any good spirits who were intermingled with them. But the multitude, excited by their leaders, reviled the angels, and rushed in upon them, for the purpose of dragging them into the forum, and treating them in an abominable manner; just as was done in Sodom. Most of them were in faith separated from charity; and there were also some who professed charity, and yet lived shamefully.

III. How the universal judgment was effected. After the visitations and premonitory signs of the coming judgment could not turn their minds from criminal acts, and from seditious plottings against those who acknowledged the Lord as the God of heaven and earth, held the Word holy, and led a life of charity, the Last Judgment came upon them. It was thus effected.

The Lord was seen in a bright cloud with angels, and a sound as of trumpets was heard from it; which was a sign representative of the protection of the angels of heaven by the Lord, and of the gathering of the good from every side. For the Lord does not bring destruction upon anyone, but only protects His own, and draws them away from communication with the evil; and when they are withdrawn, the evil come into their own lusts, and from them rush into every kind of abomination. Then all who were about to perish, were seen together like a great dragon, with its tail extended in a curve, and elevated towards heaven, bending itself about on high in various directions, as though it would destroy heaven, and draw it down. But the effort was vain, for the tail was cast down, and the dragon, which had also appeared elevated, sank down. It was granted me to see this representation, that I might know and make known who are meant by "the dragon" in the Apocalypse; namely, that "the dragon" means all who read the Word, hear preachings, and perform the holy things of the church, making no account of the lusts of evil by which they are enticed, and interiorly they meditate thefts and frauds, adulteries and obscenities, hatred and revenge, lies and blasphemies; and who thus live in spirit like devils, and in body like angels. These constituted the body of the dragon, but the tail was constituted of those who, when in the world, were in faith separated from charity, and were like the former as to thoughts and intentions.

Then I saw some of the rocks upon which they were, subsiding even to the lowest depths; some carried far away; some opening in the middle, and those who were on them cast down through the chasm; and some inundated as with a flood. And I saw many collected into companies, as into bundles, according to the genera and species of evil, and cast hither and thither into whirlpools, marshes, stagnant pools, and deserts, which were so many hells. The rest who were not on rocks, but scattered here and there, and who yet were in similar evils, fled amazed to the Papists, Mohammedans, and Gentiles, and professed their religions, which they could do without any disturbance of mind, because they had no religion; but still lest they should seduce these also, they were driven away, and thrust down to their companions in the hells. This is a general description of their destruction; the particulars which I saw, are more than can be here described.

The salvation of the sheep. After the Last Judgment was accomplished, there was then joy in heaven, and also light in the world of spirits, such as was not before. The joy in heaven and its quality, after the dragon was cast down, is described in the Apocalypse (12:10-12); and there was light in the world of spirits, because those infernal societies had been interposed like clouds which darken the earth. A similar light also then arose with men in the world, from which they had new enlightenment.

I then saw angelic spirits in great numbers rising from below, and elevated into heaven, who were the sheep, there reserved and guarded by the Lord for ages back, lest they should come into the malignant sphere flowing forth from dragonists, and their charity be suffocated. These are they, who are meant in the Word, by "those who went forth from the sepulchers"; also, by "the souls of those slain for the testimony of Jesus," who were watching; and by those "who are of the first resurrection."

CONTINUATION CONCERNING THE

SPIRITUAL WORLD. IV. THE SPIRITUAL WORLD. The spiritual world has been treated of in a special work on Heaven and Hell, in which many particulars of that world are described; and since every man enters that world after death, his state then is also described there. Who does not know that man will live after death, because he is born a man, and created in the image of God, and because the Lord, in His Word, teaches it? But what his future life will be has hitherto been unknown. It has been believed that he would then be a soul, of which no other idea was conceived than as of air or ether, in which some capacity of thought would reside, without such sight as belongs to the eye, without such hearing as belongs to the ear, and without speech such as belongs to the mouth. And yet man is equally a man after death; and such a man that he does not know otherwise than that he is still in the former world; he sees, hears, and speaks as in the former world; he walks, runs, and sits as in the former world; he eats and drinks as in the former world; he sleeps and wakes as in the former world; he enjoys conjugial delight as in the former world; in a word he is a man as to each and all things. From which it is plain, that death is but a continuation of life, and is only transition.

There are many causes why man has not known of this state of his after death; one of which is, that he could not be enlightened, so little faith had he in the immortality of the soul; as may appear from many even of the learned, who believe that they are like beasts, only more perfect than they, in being able to speak; and therefore in their heart they deny the life after death, although they profess it with the mouth. From this thought of theirs they have become so sensual, that they could not believe that a man is a man after death, because they do not see him with their eyes, for they say, how can a soul be such a man? It is otherwise with those who believe they will live after death; these think interiorly in themselves, that they will come into heaven, enjoy delights with the angels, see heavenly paradises, and stand before the Lord in white garments, besides other things. This is their interior thought; their exterior thought may wander from it, when they think of the soul from the hypothesis of the learned.

That a man is equally a man after death, although he does not appear before the eyes, may appear from the angels seen by Abraham, Gideon, Daniel, and other prophets; from the angels seen in the Lord's sepulchre, and afterwards, oftentimes, by John in the Apocalypse; especially from the Lord Himself, who showed His disciples that He was a Man, by touch, and by eating, and yet became invisible before their eyes. The reason why they saw Him was, because the eyes of their spirits were then opened; and when these are opened, the things in the spiritual world appear as clearly as the things in the natural world.

Because it has pleased the Lord to open for me the eyes of my spirit, and to keep them open now for nineteen years, it has been given me to see the things which are in the spiritual world, and also to describe them. I can affirm that they are not visions, but things seen in all wakefulness.

The difference between a man in the natural world, and a man in the spiritual world, is, that the one man is clothed with a spiritual body, but the other with a natural body; and the spiritual man sees the spiritual man, as clearly as the natural man sees the natural man; but the natural man cannot see the spiritual man, and the spiritual man cannot see the natural man, on account of the difference between the natural and the spiritual; what kind of difference this is, can be described, but not in a few words.

From the things seen during so many years, I am enabled to relate the following: that there are lands in the spiritual world, just as in the natural world; and that there are hills and mountains, plains and valleys, and also fountains and rivers, lakes and seas; there are paradises and gardens, groves and woods, and palaces and houses; also that there are writings and books, offices and trades; and that there are precious stones, gold and silver; in a word, there are each and all things that exist in the natural world, and they are infinitely more perfect in the heavens.

But the difference in general is this; that all things in the spiritual world are from a spiritual origin, and hence, as to their essence, are spiritual, they are from the sun there which is pure love; and all things in the natural world are from a natural origin, and hence as to their essence are natural, for they are from the sun there which is pure fire. Hence it is, that the spiritual man must be nourished with food from a spiritual origin, as the natural man is with food from a natural origin. More may be seen in the work on Heaven and Hell.

V. THE ENGLISH IN THE SPIRITUAL WORLD. There are two states of thought with man, an external and an internal state; man is in the external state in the natural world, in the internal state in the spiritual world: these states make one with the good, but not with the evil. What a man is as to his internal, is rarely manifest in the natural world, because from his infancy, he has wished to be moral, and has learned to seem so. But what he is, clearly appears in the spiritual world, for spiritual light discloses it, and also man is then a spirit, and the spirit is the internal man. Now, since it has been given me to be in that light, and from it, to see what the internal is in the men of various kingdoms, by an interaction of many years with angels and spirits, it behooves me to manifest it, because of its importance. Here I will say something of the noble English nation only.

The more excellent of the English nation are in the center of all Christians. The reason why they are in the center is, because they have interior intellectual light. This is not apparent to any one in the natural world, but it is conspicuous in the spiritual world. This light they derive from the liberty of thinking, and thence of speaking and of writing, in which they are. With others, who are not in such liberty, intellectual light is darkened because it has no outlet. But this light is not active of itself, but is rendered active by others, especially by men of reputation and authority among them. As soon as anything is said by these men, or as soon as anything they approve is read, that light shines forth, and seldom before. On this account governors are placed over them in the spiritual world, and priests of great reputation for learning and distinguished ability are given them, whose commands and monitions, from this their natural disposition, they cheerfully obey.

They rarely go out of their own society, because they love it as in the world they love their country. There is also a similarity of minds among them, from which they contract intimacy with friends of their own country, and rarely with others. They also mutually aid each other; and they love sincerity.

There are two great cities similar to London, into which most of the English come after death; these cities it was given me to see, as well as to walk through. The middle of the one city answers to that part of the English London where there is a meeting of merchants, called the Exchange; there the governors dwell. Above that middle is the east; below it is the west; on the right side of it is the south; on the left side of it is the north. They who have led a life of charity more than the rest, dwell in the eastern quarter, where there are magnificent palaces. The wise, with whom there are many splendid things, dwell in the southern quarter. They who more than others love the liberty of speaking and of writing, dwell in the northern quarter. They who make profession of faith, dwell in the western quarter; to the right in this quarter, there is an entrance into the city, and an exit from it; they who live wickedly are there sent out of it. The presbyters, who are in the west, and who, as was said, profess faith, dare not enter the city through the broad streets, but only through the narrower ways, because they who are in the faith of charity, are the only inhabitants who are tolerated in the city. I have heard them complaining of the preachers in the west, that they prepare their discourses with such art and at the same time eloquence, interweaving justification by faith to them unknown, that they do not know whether good is to be done or not; they preach intrinsic good, and separate it from extrinsic good, which they sometimes call meritorious, and therefore not acceptable to God; yet still they call it good, because it is useful. But when those who dwell in the eastern and southern quarters of the city hear such mystical discourses, they walk out of the temples, and the preachers are afterwards deprived of the priesthood.

The other great city similar to London, is not in the Christian center , but lies beyond it in the north. They who are interiorly evil come into it after death. In the middle of it there is an open communication with hell, by which they are swallowed up in turn.

I once heard presbyters from England conversing together concerning faith alone, and I saw a certain image made by them which represented faith alone. It appeared in obscure light like a great giant, and in their eyes like a beautiful man; but when the light of heaven was let in, the upper part of it appeared like a monster, and the lower like a serpent, not unlike the description which is given of Dagon, the idol of the Philistines. When they saw this they left it, and the bystanders cast it into a stagnant pool.

It was perceived from those of the English who are in the spiritual world, that they have as it were a twofold theology, one from the doctrine of faith, and the other from the doctrine of life; from the doctrine of faith for those who are initiated into the priesthood: from the doctrine of life for those who are not initiated into the priesthood, and who are commonly called the laity. This doctrine of life is set forth in the exhortation which is read in the temples on any Sabbath day, to those who go to the Sacrament of the Supper; in which it is openly said that if they do not shun evils as sins, they cast themselves into eternal damnation, and that if they then approach the holy communion the devil will enter into them, as he entered into Judas. I have sometimes spoken with the priests concerning this doctrine of life, that it does not agree with their doctrine of faith. They made no reply, but thought what they did not dare to utter. You may see that exhortation in The Doctrine of Life for the New

Jerusalem.

I have often seen a certain Englishman, who became celebrated by a book he published some years ago, in which he attempted to establish the conjunction of faith and charity by an influx and interior operation of the Holy Spirit. He gave out that this influx affected man in an inexpressible manner, and without his being conscious of it, but did not touch, much less manifestly move his will or excite his thought to do anything as of himself, except permissively; the reason being, that nothing of the man might enter into the Divine Providence as one with it; also that thus evils might not appear before God. He thus excluded the external exercises of charity for the sake of any salvation, but favoring them for the sake of the public good. Since his arguments were ingenious, and the snake in the grass was not seen, his book was received as most orthodox. This author retained the same dogma after his departure from the world, nor could he recede from it, because it was confirmed in him. The angels spoke with him, and said that this was not the truth, but mere ingenuity with eloquence; and that the truth is, that man ought to shun evil and do good as from himself, yet with the acknowledgment that it is from the Lord, and that there is no faith before this, still less is that thought which he calls faith. And since this was opposed to his dogma, it was permitted him of his own sagacity to inquire further, whether such unknown influx and internal operation apart from the external operation of man is given. He was then seen to strain his mind, and to wander about in thought in various ways, always in the persuasion that man is no otherwise renewed and saved. But as often as he came to the end of his way, his eyes were opened, and he saw that he was wandering, and even confessed it to those who were present. I saw him wandering thus for two years, and in the end of his ways confessing that no such influx is given, unless evil in the external man be removed, which is effected by shunning evils as sirs, as if from himself; and I heard him at length saying, that all who confirm themselves in that heresy, will be insane from the pride of their own intelligence.

I have spoken with Melancthon, and then asked him concerning his state; but he was not willing to reply. Wherefore I was informed of his lot by others, which is that he is alternately in a fretted stone chamber, and alternately in hell, and that in his chamber he appears clothed in a bear's skin on account of the cold, and because of the uncleanness there he does not admit newcomers from the world, who wish to visit him on account of the reputation of his name. He still speaks of faith alone, which in the world he established more than others.

VI. THE DUTCH IN THE SPIRITUAL WORLD. It was said above , that Christians with whom the Word is read and the Lord is worshiped, are in the middle of the nations and people of the whole spiritual world, because the greatest spiritual light is with them, and the light is radiated thence as from a center into all the circumference even to the last boundary; and it enlightens, according to what is said in The Doctrine of the New Jerusalem Concerning the Sacred Scripture. In this middle, the Reformed Christians have places allotted to them according to their reception of spiritual light from the Lord; and since the English have that light stored up in the intellectual part, therefore they are in the inmost of that middle region; and because the Dutch keep that light more nearly conjoined to natural light, and hence there is no such brightness of light apparent among them, but in its place something not transparent which is receptive of rationality from spiritual light, and at the same time from spiritual heat, they, in the Christian middle region, have obtained dwellings in the east and south; in the east from the faculty of receiving spiritual heat, which in them is charity, and in the south from the faculty of receiving spiritual light, which in them is faith. That the quarters in the spiritual world are not like the quarters in the natural world, and that dwellings according to quarters, are dwellings according to the reception of faith and love, and that they who excel in love and charity, are in the east, and they who excel in intelligence and faith, are in the south, may be seen in the work on Heaven and Hell. Another reason why they are in these quarters of the Christian middle region is, that trade is their final love, and money is the mediate subservient love, and that love is spiritual; but where money is the final love, and trade the mediate subservient love, the love is natural, and partakes of avarice. In the before-mentioned spiritual love, which regarded in itself is the common good, in which and from which is the good of the country, the Dutch excel others.

The Dutch adhere more firmly than others to the principles of their religion, nor are they drawn away from them; and if they are convinced that one or another of them is not in agreement, still they do not admit it, but turn themselves back, and remain unmoved. Thus they remove themselves from an interior intuition of truth, for they keep their rational under obedience, in spiritual things. Because they are such, when they enter the spiritual world after death, they are prepared for receiving the spiritual of heaven, which is Divine truth, quite differently from others. They are not taught, because they do not receive; but what heaven is, is described to them, and afterwards it is granted them to ascend there, and to see it; and then whatever agrees with their genius is infused into them, which being done, they are sent down, and return to their companions with a full desire for heaven. If then they do not receive this truth, that God is One in Person and in essence, and that this God is the Lord, and that in Him is the Trinity; and also this truth, that faith and charity as matters of knowledge and discourse, are of no avail apart from the life of faith and charity, and that faith and charity are given by the Lord when evils are shunned as sins; if when they are taught these truths, they turn themselves away, and still think of God as existing in three Persons, and of religion, merely that there is such a thing, they are reduced to misery, and their trade is taken away, until they are brought to the greatest extremities. And they are then led to those who have abundance of everything, and a flourishing trade, and when there, the thought is insinuated into them from heaven, whence it is that they are such, and at the same time to reflect on the faith of these persons concerning the Lord, and upon their life, in that they shun evils as sins. In a little time they make inquiries, and perceive an agreement with their own thought and reflection; this is done repeatedly. At length, they think of themselves, that in order to be relieved from their miseries, they must believe and do the same. Then, as they receive that faith, and live that life of charity, opulence and enjoyment of life are given them. In this manner, those of them who have led anything of a life of charity in the world, are amended by themselves, and not by others, and are prepared for heaven. They afterwards became more constant than others, so that they may be called constancies; and they do not allow themselves to be led away by any reasoning, fallacy, or obscurity brought on by sophistries, or by any preposterous view from confirmations alone.

The Dutch are easily distinguished from others in the spiritual world, because they appear in like garments as in the natural world, with the difference that those are in more shining ones who have received faith and that spiritual life. They appear in similar garments, because they remain constant in the principles of their religion; and in the spiritual world all are clothed according to their religious principles; whence it is, that they who are in Divine truths, have garments of white and of fine linen.

The cities in which the Dutch dwell, are guarded in a peculiar manner, all the streets in them are covered, and in the streets are gates, in order that they may not be viewed from the surrounding rocks and hills. This they do from their inherent prudence in concealing their designs, and not divulging their intentions; for these things in the spiritual world are brought forth by inspection. When anyone enters a city with the purpose of exploring their state, when he is about to depart, he is led to the closed gates of the streets, back and forth to many, and this to extreme weariness, and he is then let out; this is done to the end that he may not return. Wives who claim dominion over their husbands, dwell on one side of the city, and only meet them by invitation, given formally; and the husbands then lead them to houses, where married pairs are living, without there being any dominion of the one over the other, and show them how neat and clean their houses are, and how delightful their life is, and that these are the results of mutual and conjugial love. Those who attend to, and are affected with these things, desist from dominion, and they live together, and they then obtain a dwelling nearer to the middle, and are called angels. The reason is, that conjugial love is a celestial love, which is without dominion.

In the days of the Last Judgment, I saw many thousands of that nation cast out of the cities there, and out of the villages and surrounding lands. They were those who when in the world had done nothing of good from any religion or conscience, but only on account of reputation, that they might appear sincere for the sake of gain; for such when the prospect of fame and gain is taken away, as is the case in the spiritual world, then rush into every abomination; and when they are in the fields, and outside the cities, they rob every one they encounter. I saw them cast into a fiery gulf stretching under the eastern tract, and into a dark cavern stretching under the southern tract. This casting out I saw on the 9th day of January, 1757. Those only were left, among whom there was religion, and a conscience from religion.

I have spoken, but only once, with Calvin; he was in a society of heaven, which appears in front, above the head; and he said that he did not agree with Luther and Melancthon about faith alone, because works are so often named in the Word, and the doing of them commanded, and that therefore, faith and works ought to be conjoined. I heard from one of the governors of that society, that Calvin was accepted in his society, because he was upright and made no disturbance.

What Luther's lot is, shall be told elsewhere, for I have often heard and seen him. Here, I shall only say, that he has often wished to recede from his faith alone, but in vain; and that therefore, he is still in the world of spirits, which is midway between heaven and hell; where he sometimes suffers hard things.

VII. THE PAPISTS IN THE SPIRITUAL WORLD. The Papists, and the Last Judgment upon them, were treated of in the small work on The Last Judgment. The Papists in the spiritual world appear around the Reformed, and are separated from them by an interval, which they are not permitted to pass. Nevertheless, those who are of the order of Jesuits, by clandestine arts procure for themselves communications, and also send out emissaries, by unknown paths, for the purpose of seducing them. But they are discovered, and after being punished, they are either sent back to their companions, or are cast into hell.

After the Last Judgment, their state was so changed, that they were not allowed to gather together in companies, as before; but ways were appointed to every love, both good and evil, which those who come from the world immediately enter, and go to a society corresponding to their love. Thus the wicked are borne away to a society which is in conjunction with the hells, and the good to a society which is in conjunction with the heavens; thus precaution is taken that they may not form artificial heavens for themselves as before. Such societies in the world of spirits, which is midway between heaven and hell, are innumerable; being as many as there are genera and species of good and evil affections. And in the meantime, before spirits are either elevated into heaven, or cast down into hell, they are in spiritual conjunction with men in the world, because they too are in the midst between heaven and hell.

All those of the Papists, who have not been wholly idolaters, and who, from their religious persuasion, have done goods out of a sincere heart, and have also looked to the Lord, are led to societies which are instituted in the confines nearest to the Reformed, and are instructed there, the Word being read, and the Lord preached to them; and they who receive truths and apply them to life, are elevated into heaven and become angels. There are many such societies of them in every quarter, and they are guarded on all sides from the treacheries and cunning devices of the monks, and from the Babylonish leaven. Moreover, all their infants are in heaven, because, being educated by the angels under the guidance of the Lord, they know nothing of the falsities of the religion of their parents.

All who come from the earth into the spiritual world, are at first kept in the confession of faith, and in the religion of their country; and so therefore are the Papists. On this account, they always have some representative Pontiff set over them, whom they also adore with the same ceremony as in the world. Rarely does any Pope from the world act the Pontiff there; yet he who was Pope at Rome twenty years ago, was appointed over the Papists, because he cherished in heart that the Word is more holy than is believed, and that the Lord ought to be worshiped. But, after filling the office of Pope for some years, he abdicated it, and betook himself to the Reformed Christians, among whom he still is, and enjoys a happy life. It was granted me to speak with him, and he said, that he adored the Lord alone, because He is God, who has power over heaven and earth, and that the invocations of saints, and also their masses, are trifles; and that when he was in the world, he intended to restore that church, but that for reasons, which he mentioned, he found it impossible to do so. When the great northern city of the Papists was destroyed, on the day of the Last Judgment, I saw him carried out of it on a couch, and taken to a place of safety. Quite a different thing happened to his successor.

Here I am allowed to add something memorable. It was granted me to speak with Louis XIV., grandfather of the reigning king of France, who while he was in the world, worshiped the Lord, read the Word, and acknowledged the Pope only as the highest one of the church; in consequence of which, he has great dignity in the spiritual world, and rules the best society of the French nation. Once I saw him as it were descending by ladders, and after he descended I heard him saying, that he seemed to himself as if at Versailles, and then there was silence round about for half an hour; at the end of that time, he said, that he had spoken with the king of France, his grandson, concerning the Bull Unigenitus, advising him to desist from his former design, and not to accept it, because it was detrimental to the French nation, he said that he insinuated this into his thought profoundly. This took place in the year 1759, on the 13th day of December, about eight o'clock in the evening.

VIII. THE POPISH SAINTS IN THE SPIRITUAL WORLD. It is known that man has from his parents implanted or hereditary evil, but in what it consists is known to few. It consists in the love of ruling, which is such, that as far as the reins are given it, so far it bursts forth, until it even burns with the lust of ruling over all, and at length of wishing to be invoked and worshiped as God. This love is the serpent, which deceived Eve and Adam, for it said to the woman: God knows, that in the day ye eat of the fruit of the tree, your eyes shall be opened, and then ye shall be as God (Gen. 3:4, 5). As far therefore as man rushes with loosened reins into this love, so far he turns himself away from God, and turns towards himself, and becomes an atheist; and then the Divine truths which are of the Word, may serve as means, but because dominion is the end, the means are in the heart only as they serve him. This is the reason why those who are in the mediate and in the ultimate degree of the love of ruling, are all in hell, for that love is the devil there; and in hell there are some of such a nature, that they cannot bear to hear any one speaking of God.

Those of the Papal nation have this love who have had dominion from the frenzy of its delight, and have despised the Word, and preferred the dictates of the Pope to it. They are utterly devastated as to externals, until they no longer know anything of the church, and then they are cast down into hell and become devils. There is a certain separate hell for those who wish to be invoked as gods, where such is their fantasy, that they do not see what is, but what is not. Their delirium is such as affects persons in a malignant fever, who see things floating in the air and in the chamber, and on the covering of the bed, which do not exist. This worst of evils is meant by: The head of the serpent, which is bruised by the Seed of the woman, and which wounds His heel (Gen. 3:15). "The heel" of the Lord, who is "the Seed of the woman," is the Divine proceeding in ultimates, which is the Word in the sense of the letter.

Because man from heredity is such, that he wishes to rule, and as the reins are loosened, successively over more, and at length over all, and because the wish to be invoked and worshiped as

God, is the inmost of this love of ruling, therefore all who have been made saints by the Papal bulls, are removed from the sight of others and hidden, and are deprived of all interaction with their worshipers. This is done, lest that worst root of evils should be excited in them, and they should be hurried into such fantastic deliriums as prevail in the above mentioned hell. In such deliriums are those who, when they lived in the world, have eagerly sought to be made saints after death, for the purpose of being invoked.

Many of the Papal nation, especially the monks, when they come into the spiritual world, seek the saints, each the saint of his own order; yet they do not find them, and therefore they wonder. But afterwards they are instructed by others, that they are either intermingled with those who are in the heavens, or with those who are in the hells, every one according to his life in the world; and that in whichsoever they are, they know nothing of the worship and invocation of themselves; and that they who know it, and wished to be invoked, are in that separate and delirious hell. The worship of saints is such an abomination in heaven, that whenever they hear of it they are horrified, because as far as worship is paid to any man, in so far it is withheld from the Lord, for thus He alone cannot be worshiped; and if the Lord is not alone worshiped, a discrimination is made, which destroys communion, and the felicity of life which flows from it.

That I might know, for the sake of informing others, what kind of men the Popish saints are, as many as a hundred of them, who knew of their canonization, were brought up from the lower earth. The greater part ascended from behind, and only a few in front, and I spoke with one of them, who they said was Xavier. While he talked with me, he was quite foolish, yet he was able to tell me, that in his place, where he remains confined, he is not so; but that he becomes foolish as often as he thinks that he is a saint. I heard a like murmur from those who were behind.

It is otherwise with the so-called saints who are in heaven; they know nothing at all of what is doing upon earth, nor have I spoken with them, lest any idea of this should enter their minds. Only once Mary, the mother of the Lord, passed by, and appeared over head in white raiment, and then, stopping awhile, she said that she had been the mother of the Lord, and that He was indeed born of her, but that He became God, and put off all the human from her, and that therefore she now adores Him as her God, and is unwilling that any one should acknowledge Him as her Son, because in Him all is Divine.

I will here add this Relation. A certain woman in splendid raiment and with saint-like countenance, occasionally appears in a middle altitude, to the Parisians who are in a society in the spiritual world, and tells them she is Genevieve. But as soon as any of them begin to adore her, then instantly her countenance is changed, and her raiment too, and she becomes like an ordinary woman, and chides them for wishing to adore a woman, who, among her companions, is in no more repute than a maid servant; wondering that men in the world are caught by such trifles. The angels said that she appears for the purpose of separating those there who worship man from those who worship the Lord.

IX. THE MOHAMMEDANS IN THE SPIRITUAL WORLD; AND MOHAMMED. The Mohammedans in the spiritual world appear behind the Papists in the west, and form as it were a circle around them. The principal reason why they appear there is, because they acknowledge the Lord as the Greatest Prophet, the Son of God, the Wisest of all, who was sent into the world to teach men. Every one in that world dwells at a distance from the Christian center where the Reformed are, according to his confession of the Lord and of one God; for that confession conjoins minds with heaven, and determines distance from the east, above which the Lord is. They who, from the life of evil, are not in that confession in heart, are in the hells beneath them.

Since religion makes man's inmost, and all the rest proceeds from the inmost, and since Mohammed is closely connected with their religion, therefore some Mohammed is always placed in their sight; and in order that they may turn their faces to the east, above which the Lord is, he is placed beneath in the Christian center. It is not the Mohammed himself who wrote the Koran, but another who fills his office; nor is it always the same, but he is changed. Once it was one from Saxony, who had been taken by the Algerians, and became a Mohammedan; and who, having been also a Christian, was actuated to speak to them concerning the Lord, that He was not the Son of Joseph, as they believed in the world, but the Son of God Himself, by which he insinuated into them an idea of the unity of the Lord's Person and Essence with the Father. To this Mohammed, others afterwards succeeded, who were actuated to declare the same. By this means, many of them accede to a truly Christian faith concerning the Lord, and they who do so accede, are carried to a society nearer to the east, where communication is granted them from heaven, into which they are afterwards elevated. In the place where the seat of that Mohammed is, there appears a fire like a torch, that he may be known, but it is invisible to all but Mohammedans.

Mohammed himself, who wrote the Koran, is not to be seen at the present day. I was told, that in early times he presided over the Mohammedans, but because be wished to domineer over all things of their religion as a God, he was cast out of his seat which he held beneath the Papists, and was sent downwards, to the right side near the south. Once some societies of Mohammedans were excited by the malicious to acknowledge Mohammed as God. To quell the sedition, Mohammed was raised up from below and shown to them, and then I also saw him. He appeared like corporeal spirits, who have no interior perception, his face approaching to black; and I heard him saying these words only, "I am your Mohammed;" and soon sinking down, as it were, he returned to his place.

As regards their religion, it was permitted such as it is, because of its agreement with the genius of the Orientals, on which account, too, it was received in so many kingdoms; and because, at the same time, it made the precepts of the Decalogue a matter of religion, and it had something from the Word, and especially because it acknowledged the Lord as the Son of God, and the wisest of all. And besides it dissipated the idolatries of many nations. The reason why Mohammed was not made the means of opening to his followers a more interior religion, was on account of polygamy, which exhales uncleanness towards heaven; for the marriage of a husband with one wife, corresponds to the marriage of the Lord and the Church.

Many of them are receptive of truth, and they see

justice in reasons, as I was enabled to observe from conversations with them in the spiritual world. I spoke with them concerning the One God, the resurrection, and marriage. Of the One God they said, that they do not comprehend the Christians when speaking of the Trinity, and saying that there are three Persons, and that each Person is God, and still saying that God is one. But I replied, that the angels in the heaven which is from Christians, do not speak thus, but say, that God is one in essence and in Person, and in whom is a Trine, and that men on earth call this Trine three Persons; and that this Trine is in the Lord. In confirmation, I read before them out of Matthew and Luke, all that is said there of the conception of the Lord from God the Father, as well as the passages in which He Himself teaches, that He and the Father are one. On hearing this they perceived it, saying that thus the Divine essence is in Him. Of the Resurrection they said, that they do not comprehend Christians when they speak of the state of man after death, making the soul like wind or air, and hence is deprived of all delight before its reunion with the body at the day of the Last Judgment. But I replied, that only some talk thus, but that they who are not of that class, believe they will come into heaven after death, will speak with the angels, and enter upon heavenly joy, which they do not conceive to be dissimilar to their joy in the world, although they do not describe it; and I told them, that at the present day, many particulars of the state after death are revealed to them, which they did not know before. Of Marriage, I have had many conversations with them, and have told them, among other things, that conjugial love is a celestial love, which can exist only between two, and that conjunction with many wives does not admit the celestial of that love. They heard my reasons, and perceived their justice; as also this, that polygamy was permitted them, because they are Orientals, who without this permission would have burned for foul adulteries more than Europeans, and would have perished.

X. THE AFRICANS AND THE GENTILES IN THE SPIRITUAL WORLD. The Gentiles who know nothing concerning the Lord, appear around those who know of Him; so that no others make the extreme circumferences but those who are altogether idolatrous, and have adored the sun and moon. But they who acknowledge one God, and make precepts like those of the Decalogue a part of religion and of life, are seen in a higher region, and thus communicate more immediately with the Christians in the center; for thus the communication is not intercepted by the Mohammedans and Papists. The Gentiles are also distinguished according to their genius and faculty of receiving light through the heavens from the Lord; for there are some of them who are more interior, and some who are more exterior; and these diversities are not derived from their place of birth, but from their religion. The Africans are more interior than the rest.

All who acknowledge and worship one God, the Creator of the universe, have concerning Him the idea of Man: they say, that concerning God, no one can have any other idea. When they hear that many cherish the idea of Him as of a small cloud, they inquire where they are, and on being told that they are among Christians, they deny the possibility of it. But it is replied, that Christians have this idea, because God in the Word is called Spirit, and of a spirit, they are accustomed to think that it is like a particle of cloud, not knowing that every spirit and every angel is a man. Yet when they were explored, to discover whether their spiritual and natural ideas were alike, it was found that they were not alike with those who interiorly acknowledge the Lord as the God of heaven and earth. I heard a certain presbyter of the Christians saying, that no one can have an idea of the Divine Human; and I saw him led about to various Gentiles, in succession to those who were more and more interior, and from them to their heavens, and at length to the Christian heaven, and the interior perception of all concerning God was communicated to him, and he perceived that their idea of God was no other than the idea of Man, which is the same as the idea of the Divine Human.

There are many societies of Gentiles, especially from the Africans, who, on being instructed by the angels concerning the Lord, say that it cannot be otherwise than that God the Creator of the universe should appear in the world, because He created them and loves them; and that the appearance must be made before the very eyes in the Human form. When they are told, that He did not appear as the angels are wont to appear, but that He was born Man, and thus became visible, they hesitate awhile, and inquire whether He was born from a human father; and on hearing that he was conceived by the God of the universe, and born of a virgin, they say that thus He has the Divine essence itself, which because it is infinite and life itself, He was not such a man as others are. They are afterwards informed by the angels, that in aspect He was like another man, but that when He was in the world, His Divine essence, which in itself is infinite and life itself, rejected the finite nature and its life from the mother, and thus made His Human, which was conceived and born in the world, Divine. The Africans comprehended and received these things, because they think more interiorly and spiritually than others.

Such being the character of the Africans even in the world, there is, at the present day, a revelation with them, which commencing in the center, is communicated around, but does not reach the seas. They acknowledge our Lord as the God of heaven and earth, and laugh at the monks in those parts they visit, and at the Christians who talk of a three-fold Divinity, and of salvation by mere thinking, saying, that there is no man who has any worship, who does not live according to his religion, and that whosoever does not, must become stupid and wicked, because then he receives nothing from heaven. Ingenious wickedness they also call stupidity, because in it there is not life but death. I have heard the angels rejoicing over this revelation, because, by means of it, a communication is opened for them with the human rational, hitherto closed up by the blindness which has been drawn over the things of faith. It was told me from heaven, that the truths now published in The Doctrine of the New Jerusalem Concerning the Lord, Concerning the Word, and in The Doctrine of Life for the New Jerusalem, are orally dictated by angelic spirits to the inhabitants of that country.

When I spoke with the Africans in the spiritual world, they appeared in striped garments of linen: they said that such garments correspond to them, and that their women have striped garments of silk. Of their little children, they related, that they frequently ask their nurses for food, saying that they are hungry, and when food is set before them, they examine and taste whether it agrees with them, and eat but little; whence it is evident, that spiritual hunger, which is a desire of knowing genuine truths, produces this effect; for it is a correspondence When the Africans wish to know their state as to the affection and perception of truth, they draw their swords; and if these shine, they know that they are in genuine truths, in a degree according to the shining; this, too, is from correspondence. Of marriage they said, that it is indeed allowed them by law to have several wives, but that still they take but one, because love truly conjugial is not divided; and that if it is divided, its essence which is heavenly perishes, and it becomes external and thence lascivious, and in a short time grows vile, as its potency diminishes, and at length is loathed when the potency is lost; but love truly conjugial, which is internal, and derives nothing from lasciviousness, remains to eternity, and increases in potency, and in the same degree in delight.

Strangers from Europe they said, are not admitted, and when any penetrate into their country, especially monks, they ask them what they know, and when they relate any particulars of their religious persuasion, they call them trifles which offend their very ears, and they then send them out of the way to work, in order that they may do something useful; and if they refuse to work, they sell them for slaves, whom their law allows them to chastise at will; and if they cannot drive them to do anything useful, they are at last sold for a small sum to the lowest class.

XI. THE JEWS IN THE SPIRITUAL WORLD. Before the Last Judgment the Jews appeared in a valley in the spiritual world, at the left side of the Christian center; but after it, they were transferred into the north, and forbidden to hold interaction with

Christians, except with those who wandered outside the cities. In that quarter, there are two great cities into which the Jews are led after death, and which before the judgment, were called Jerusalems, but after it by another name, because after the judgment by "Jerusalem" is meant the church in which the Lord alone is adored. In these cities, converted Jews are appointed over them, who admonish them not to speak scoffingly of Christ; and punish those who still do so. The streets of their cities are filled with mire up to the ankles, and their houses are full of uncleanness, from which they smell, so that they cannot be approached.

An angel sometimes appears to them in a middle altitude above them, with a rod in his hand, and gives them to believe that he is Moses, and exhorts them to desist from the madness of expecting the Messiah even there, because Christ, who governs them and all other men, is the Messiah: he says, that he knows it to be so, and also, that when he was in the world, he knew something concerning Him. On hearing this, they retire; the chief part of them forgetting, and only a few retaining it. They who do retain it are sent to synagogues, which are composed of the converted, and are there instructed; and if they receive instruction, they have new garments given them in place of their old tattered ones, and are presented with the Word neatly written, and with a dwelling in a not unsightly city. But they who do not receive, are cast down into the hells, beneath their great tract; many also are cast into forests and into deserts, where they commit robberies among themselves.

In that world, as in the former, they traffic in various things, especially in precious stones, which, by unknown ways, they procure for themselves from heaven, where there are precious stones in abundance. The reason of their trading in precious stones is, that they read the Word in its original language, and regard the sense of its letter as holy, and precious stones correspond to the sense of the letter of the Word. On the subject of this correspondence, see The Doctrine of the New Jerusalem Concerning the Sacred Scripture. They sell their precious stones to the Gentiles who encircle them in the northern quarter. They also have the art of producing imitations, and of inducing the fancy that they are genuine; but they who do so are heavily fined by their governors.

The Jews are more ignorant than others as to their being in the spiritual world, believing that they are still in the natural world. The reason is, that they are wholly external men, and do not think at all of their religion from the interior. On this account also they speak of the Messiah just as they did before, as that He will come with David, and will go before them glittering with diadems, and introduce them into the land of Canaan; and that in the way, by lifting His rod, He will dry up the rivers which they will pass over; and that Christians, whom among themselves they call Gentiles, will then lay hold of the skirts of their garments, and humbly entreat to be allowed to accompany them, and that they will receive the rich according to their wealth, and that even the rich are to serve them. For they are unwilling to know, that "the land of Canaan" in the Word, means the church, and "Jerusalem," the church as to doctrine; and hence that "Jews" mean all those who will be of the Lord's church. That such is the meaning of "Jews" in the Word, may be seen in The Doctrine Concerning the Sacred Scripture. When they are asked, whether they believe that they also are to enter the land of Canaan, they reply, that they will then descend into it. When it is said, that this land cannot possibly hold them all, they reply that it will then be enlarged. When it is said that they do not know where Bethlehem is nor who is of the stock of David, they say, that it is known to the Messiah who is to come. When asked, how the Messiah the Son of Jehovah, can dwell with those who are so evil, they reply that they are not evil. When it is said that still Moses describes them in his song (Deut. 32) as the worst of nations, they answer, that Moses at that time was angry, because he was to die. But when they are told, that Moses wrote it by the command of Jehovah, they are silent, and go away to consult about the matter. When it is said, that they took their origin from a Canaanite, and from the whoredom of Judah with his daughter-in-law (Gen. 38), they are enraged, and say, that it suffices them to be descended from Abraham. When they are told that interiorly in the Word there is a spiritual sense, which treats of Christ alone, they reply, that it is not so, but that interiorly in the Word there is nothing but gold; besides many such things.

XII. THE QUAKERS IN THE SPIRITUAL WORLD. There are enthusiastic spirits, separated from all others, of such gross perception, that they believe themselves to be the Holy Spirit. When Quakerism commenced, these spirits, being drawn out as it were from encircling forests where they were wandering, obsessed many; infusing the persuasion that they were moved by the Holy Spirit; and because they perceived the influx sensibly, they became so completely filled with this kind of religious persuasion, that they believed themselves more enlightened and holier than the rest; therefore also they could not be withdrawn from their religious persuasion. They who have confirmed themselves therein, come into a similar enthusiasm after death, and are separated from the rest, and sent away to their like in forests, where, at a distance, they appear like wild swine. But they who have not confirmed themselves, being separated from the others, are remanded to a place like a desert, in the extreme borders of the southern quarter, where they have caves for their temples.

After the former enthusiastic spirits were removed from them, the trembling which from these spirits had seized their bodies ceased, and they now feel a motion in their left side. It was shown, that from the first time they have gone successively into worse things, and at length, by command of their holy spirit, into heinous things, which they divulge to no one. I conversed with the founder of their religious persuasion, and with Penn, who said that they had no part in such things. But they who have perpetrated such things, are sent down after death into a dark place, where they sit in corners, appearing like the dregs of oil.

Since they have rejected the two sacraments, Baptism and the Holy Supper, and still read the Word, and preach the Lord, and speak obsessed by enthusiastic spirits, and thus commix the holy things of the Word with truths profaned, therefore no society is formed of them in the spiritual world, but after being dissociated they wander hither and thither, and are dispersed, and gathered into the above mentioned desert.

XIII. THE MORAVIANS IN THE SPIRITUAL WORLD. I have conversed much with the Moravians, who are also called Herrnhuters. They appeared, at first, in a valley not far from the Jews;

but after being examined and detected, were conveyed away into uninhabited places. When they were being examined, they knew how with cunning to captivate minds, saying, that they were the remains of the Apostolic Church, and that therefore they salute each other as brethren, and those who receive their interior mysteries as mothers; also that they teach faith better than others and love the Lord because He suffered the cross, calling Him the Lamb, and the Throne of grace; with other like expressions, by which they induce the belief that the Christian church itself is with them. Those who are captivated by their smooth speeches and draw near to them, are examined by them to see whether they are such that they dare disclose to them their mysteries; if not they conceal them; if they can they reveal them; and then they warn and also threaten those who divulge their mystery concerning the Lord.

Since they did the same in the spiritual world, when yet it was perceived that interiorly they did not think so, in order that this might be disclosed, they were admitted into the lowest heaven; but they did not endure the sphere of the charity and faith of the angels there, and they fled away. Afterwards, because in the world they believed that they alone would be alive, and would enter the third heaven, they were also carried up into this heaven, but on perceiving the sphere of love to the Lord there, they were seized with anguish of heart, and began to suffer interior tortures, and to move convulsively, like those who are in the agony of death, therefore they cast themselves down headlong thence. In this manner it was first made manifest that inwardly they had cherished nothing of charity toward the neighbor, and nothing of love to the Lord. They were afterwards sent to those whose function it is to examine the interiors of the thoughts, and these said of them, that they hold the Lord in little estimation, that they reject the life of charity so as to abhor it, and that they make the Word of the Old Testament useless, and despise the Word of the Evangelists; only of their good pleasure selecting from Paul, where anything is said of faith alone; and that these are their mysteries, which they conceal from the world.

After it was made manifest that they acknowledge the Lord only as the Arians do, that they despise the Word of the Prophets and Evangelists, and hold a life of charity in hatred, when yet upon these three things as on pillars the whole heaven depends; then they who were in the knowledge and at the came time in the belief of their mysteries, were adjudged Anti-Christs, who reject the three essentials of the Christian church, namely, the Divine of the Lord, the Word, and charity, and were cast outside the Christian world into a desert, which is in the end of the southern quarter near the Quakers.

When Zinzendorf first came into the spiritual world after death, and was permitted to speak as before in the world, I heard him asserting, that he knew the mysteries of heaven, and that no one enters heaven who is not of his doctrine; and also, that they who do good works for the sake of salvation, are utterly damned, and that he would rather admit atheists into his congregation than them. The Lord, he said, was adopted by God the Father as His Son, because He endured the cross, and that still He was simply a man. When it was said to him, that the Lord was conceived by God the Father, he replied, that he thought of that matter as he chose, not daring to speak out as the Jews do. Moreover, I have perceived many scandals from his followers, when I have been reading the Evangelists.

They say, that they have a sensation, and thence an interior confirmation of their dogmas. But it was shown to them, that their sensation was from visionary spirits, who confirm a man in all his religious persuasions, and enter more closely with those, who like the Moravians, love their religious persuasion, and think much concerning it. These spirits also talked with them, and they mutually recognized each other.

www.ingramcontent.com/pod-product-compliance
Lightning Source LLC
Chambersburg PA
CBHW021914040426
42447CB00007B/856